ROOTED IN HUMANITY
Reclaiming Benevolence in Support of a Community's Coming of Age

ROOTED IN HUMANITY
Reclaiming Benevolence in Support of a Community's Coming of Age

By
Lori Ann

Contributions: Natasha Warsaw and Members of
the first Benevolent Community Cohort

In Remembrance of Ouida Watson

It is with deep sorrow that we honor the loss of a dear member of our Benevolent Community Circle...

Ouida was a good friend, committed to making this world a better place, and a treasured member of our Benevolent Community Circle. Our community is about connection, shared humanity, kindness, and carrying one another's stories. Ouida's voice will be dearly missed, but her stories and her heart will continue to live on in each of us and in our community.
May her memory always be for a blessing.

Rooted In Humanity:
Reclaiming Benevolence in Support of a
Community's Coming of Age
Copyright © 2025
Lori Ann

Comments:
4hoping@gmail.com

ISBN:
979-8-218-82259-0

Published by
still learning, inc.

Table of Contents:

Introduction:

A few opening thoughts about this book and the Benevolent Community Initiative that has emerged through our engagement with these ideas and cultivated in the year long conversations held with the first Benevolent Community Circle Cohort...

From Natasha -

The opportunity to be a part of and support this beautiful community has been a gift. It began as the seed of an idea and out of my need to find a way to contribute to bridging the divides that continue to plague our country. We began this work in the midst of the COVID-19 crisis and a need for community and connection at a time when so many were isolated made the work feel imperative. Lori and I have known each other for a number of years through our work as independent facilitators with the Center for Courage and Renewal, and when I started to formulate plans for the group, I knew that she was the perfect person to partner with.

Our journey has been one of trial and error, however over the last two years, in concert with the beautiful community that we've been a part of building, we have found a formula that works. It has been an amazing experience, and it is one that we hope that others across the country will have the opportunity to experience. That is the purpose of this book.

We hope that after reading this, and delving into the perspectives and experiences of our community members, you will not only appreciate the community that we have built, but we also hope that you will be inspired to build your own. We are excited for you, and we look forward to walking each step of the way with you.

From Lori -

I humbly add a few thoughts to Natasha's words of introduction - I am called to work and research that exists at the intersections of humanity, community, integrity, and benevolence. My aim is to witness human interaction and listen to lived experiences to understand how to best harness the interconnected space between these threads. When woven together, they create a life-force for unity, dignity, empathy, compassion, and good. The root of the word "benevolence" is "bene," meaning "I wish you well." My aspiration to walk this path and create a benevolent community stem from my desire to live in a humane centered environment that embodies "wishing each other well" as a daily sacred practice – a true habit of the heart. I am convinced that when we achieve this together, we will illuminate the gifts of our shared humanity, nourishing a profound shift in how we see each other, listen to, respond, and interact with each other. In such a moment, a deep commitment to fostering genuine connection and mutual support will blossom, and a true benevolent community will be born.

None of this would have flourished without the trust and friendship I developed with my dear colleague, Natasha. Thankfully, she reached out to me and invited me to journey with her during the challenging and isolating times of the COVID-19 pandemic. Together, with a beautiful group of souls willing to embrace the ambiguity of a journey without a clear destination, we grew into a benevolent community, one that truly understands and cares for each other. Despite our individual differences, our work together has illuminated our shared humanity, highlighting our unique qualities and inherent gifts.

We welcome you to join us! We believe that together we can build communities that uplift and honor each other while committing to the idea that just as individuals mature and "come of age," so can an intentional community. We hope this book will be held as a gentle guide, and that our experience will inspire and motivate you to join us in building a path to benevolent human relationships that are the only thing we know of to live into the ideal of creating and sustaining a more perfect union between all people.

We Acknowledge with Love –

We wish to extend our heartfelt thanks to one of our beloved mentors, **Parker J. Palmer**, for his profound wisdom and his approach to human connection and integrity, which have deeply influenced our work. Parker, we both feel so fortunate to have had you as a teacher, mentor, and most grateful to you for years of being blessed with your generosity of heart and friendship.

We also thank our dear friends and colleagues at the **Center for Courage & Renewal®** for their camaraderie and support. To learn more about the work and books of Parker J. Palmer, or the wonderful programs provided by the Center for Courage & Renewal you can contact them at: https://couragerenewal.org

With deep gratitude, we honor the members of the first Benevolent Community Circle Cohort—your commitment and courage made this journey possible. We appreciate those of you who contributed your words, ideas, and heart to this work. How wonderful it is to have you in our lives, a part of our community and extended family. To **Candy, Clint, Denise, Joe, Kathie, Marlene, Monica, Ouida, Sally, and Shenita** – we share this book, our deep respect, and heartfelt thanks.

Many thanks to our friend and the talented artist who created the beautiful cover of this book – **Karen Rauppius** – we love how you captured the essence of our writing in this beautiful tree whose exposed roots remind us to always root ourselves in humanity, using the human values that center us, steady us, and keep us on the path to benevolent community.

My sincere and deep gratitude to **Bob O'Brien,** publisher extraordinaire. Bob so patiently and graciously shepherded me through my first book, and I feel fortunate that he once again supported both this book and my children's book which with his guidance and help went from pages on my computer to beautiful books in my hands. Thank you, Bob!

Every book needs a testimonial – one or more close readers, often those we greatly admire and trust to provide an honest review while also adding their authentic voice. I am so grateful to my dear friend, **Jim Rogers**, whose work, wisdom and writing I have held with deep regard for so many years. I feel honored to have his thoughts and his long view - 90 years of listening and witnessing grace the back cover of this book.

We also humbly offer thanks to all who over these years of development have supported our work in so many ways of giving. Your generosity lifted our spirits and allowed us to continue to build the framework for the Benevolent Community Initiative.

And finally, we offer a deep bow of respect, appreciation, and love to **Sally Z. Hare**—a friend, mentor, teacher, and active member of our Benevolent Community Circle, and to **Dave Ellis**, a dear friend and colleague who has provided perspective, insight, and his time and experience to co-facilitate the Healing History Retreats, one of our Benevolent Community Initiative offerings.

Sally is an Elder in the truest sense - not defined by age, but by deep-seated wisdom, generosity, and integrity. Her book, *The ElderGarten: A Field Guide for the Journey of a Lifetime*, profoundly shaped our understanding of the essential role of Elders as leaders, truth-tellers, listeners, and trusted guides in the effort to build communities worthy of our humanity. We highly recommend, Sally's book, The ElderGarten: A Field Guide for the Journey of a Lifetime, she is an engaging speaker and thought leader and can be reached at: couragetoteach@sc.rr.com

Dave is a gifted communicator and wise soul who has so graciously provided his expertise in the field of trauma and his model, The 5-Fold Path to Healing ™, that has become essential to how we approach being in Benevolent Community Circles with each other and has enlightened our Healing History Retreats with the grounding and understanding integral to bringing a broader lens to the interconnectedness of humanity, community, history, compassion, and healing.

Natasha and I are available to consulst and support those interested in beginning a Benevolent Community Circle or holding a Benevolent Community Retreat or workshop. Dave and Lori welcome you to explore the Healing History Retreat opportunities. Please contact Lori for additional information at director@createsafespace.org.

It is our sincere hope that this book, its reflections, thought work, and invitations to practice will support your heart, inspire your soul, and uplift hope. We believe that together we can build communities worthy of our shared humanity.

With sincere gratitude, Lori Ann - Natasha Warsaw

May the thoughts and questions here take root in your community, and may the path you create be one that reclaims the gifts of our shared humanity -benevolence, integrity, humility, generosity, compassion, and belonging.

Dedication

With my whole heart, I dedicate this book to my children and grandchildren (A,R, J,R, M,J, S,T, R, A, E, I) who inspire me with their kindness and courage, and to my dear D.L. — your presence in my life brings me joy and light, comfort and hope even on the stormiest of days. I have learned to acknowledge the need to cling to the roots of our Ancestors whose stories, lessons, and warnings are wrapped in meaning, concern, and love for life.

This book is my way of sharing my lived experiences and observations - and my hopeful resolve that together we can build communities

worthy of our shared humanity.

Lori Ann

Preface: The Rise and Fall of Benevolence and the Call to Community

We are, by nature, communal beings. From our earliest days, humans have gathered - around fires, under trees, in circles, and in sanctuaries - to share food, wisdom, laughter, stories, and sorrow. Our communities have shaped us, held us, taught us how to be with one another. In our best moments, they have called forth our greatest virtues: compassion, empathy, kindness, generosity, and trust.

And yet history, like the tide, has shown us the rise and fall of these ideals. There have been periods - some ancient, some recent - when the spirit of benevolence ran strong, animating civic life, spiritual tradition, and social responsibility. And there have been times when doubt, division, and dehumanization hollowed out the very core of our communal life.

It is my belief that one reason benevolence within community, and community itself, has not always endured is that we have failed to recognize the value of a process by which a community matures.
Just as human beings grow through stages of development, communities too require care, reflection, and intention to evolve. Without a shared process of learning, healing, and growing, communities remain divided, stalled in cycles of reaction instead of becoming grounded in relational trust and collective wisdom.

We are now living in a time of deep fragmentation. Though more "connected" than ever before, we find ourselves drifting farther from one another. The rise of digital technology - smartphones, social media, and the constant presence of online life - has reshaped how we relate to ourselves and one another.

In the rush to stay informed and constantly reachable,

we have too often replaced presence with performance, depth with reaction, and belonging with algorithm-driven affirmation.

We are witnessing the slow erosion of our ability to truly see one another - with empathy, dignity, and care. The sacred art of human interaction has dimmed, and with it, our sense of shared responsibility for the well-being of the whole.

And yet, I believe something deeper remains - a pulse, a memory, an ache for the kind of community that nourishes the soul and strengthens the social fabric. This book is rooted in that belief.

Rooted in Humanity is both a reflection and a call to action. It offers a blueprint - woven from lived experience, ethical inquiry, and the stories of those who have dared to ask essential questions for building communities that are not only inclusive, but worthy of our humanity. Communities shaped by integrity, compassion, generosity, and trust. Communities that hold space for difference, wrestle with truth, and commit to one another's well-being.

A Benevolent Community is not a nostalgic return to the past. It is a complete recentering and a necessary act of reclaiming what it means to be human - together. It is an invitation to cultivate maturity within our shared lives. To foster a *community's coming of age*, where our care for one another expands alongside our capacity for truth-telling, repair, and belonging.

There is no more urgent work.

Beneath all the noise, the heart still longs to be held in community, let us answer that longing with intention, with integrity, and with love.

 LORI ANN

As you begin to engage with the pages of this book, I invite you to carry two rooted ideas that I have found integral to growing benevolent community…

Trust and Safety Walk Hand In Hand:

Trust is central to the foundational human need for external (physical, relational) and internal (emotional, spiritual) safety.

Sensing that we are safe provides our mind, heart, body, and spirit with the necessary time to rest and re-energize so to:

- Fully engage with the whole of ourselves and others,
- Rationally and critically reflect on life, our situations, challenges, failures, and successes to discern opportunities, choices, possibilities, solutions, consequences, and outcomes,
- And to wonder, imagine, dream, create and build our life in ways that are aligned with our values and moral code of ethics that supports our well-being and upholds our humanity.

Trusting that we are safe "enough" in our physical environment, our relationships, and our emotional, spiritual, and intellectual space is necessary for human beings to feel stable and secure - to move from "surviving to thriving".

Trust (in oneself and others) is the key element, ingredient, and factor needed for human beings to thrive, to live with dignity and integrity, to self-actualize and fully illuminate the gifts of humanity.

We cannot hope for positive outcomes without living into the truth of needing to build safe environments that honor the internal and external human need for trust-worthy spaces so to live integrally, holding others'

dignity equal to our own.

My wise friend, Sally Z. Hare reminds us that,

"Learning to trust (or not) is the child's first work --- and the results of this all-important work affects the rest of their lives".

Essential Questions deepen understanding of our individual and collective journey needed to ignite community transformation.

In our journey toward building Benevolent Communities, one of the most transformative tools we wield is not answers - but the questions we dare to ask. As Elizabeth Weingarten reminds us in her book, *How to Fall in Love with Questions*, real growth "often arises not from finding answers, but from loving and living within the questions," nurturing "curiosity, emotional awareness, and self-compassion" allows us to move forward with clarity, perseverance, and a deeper connection to ourselves and others.

This practice is not just an individual endeavor but a communal one, integral and essential to how we hold spaces of authenticity and mutual understanding. As Weingarten reinterprets Ranier Maria Rilke's enduring wisdom: "Be patient about everything that is still unresolved in your heart; try to love the questions themselves, like locked rooms, like books written in a truly foreign language." Such patience invites us to inhabit ambiguity not with fear, but with compassion - for ourselves and for the unfolding stories within our communities.

In our current cultural climate, where certainty is often overvalued, Weingarten offers a vital corrective to: "approach uncertainty with curiosity rather than fear..." —

17

mirroring our held belief that turning to wonder opens us to new perspectives and each other.

Asking essential questions is integral to the Benevolent Community process, which invites participants to step into spaces of not knowing together - where honest essential questions, held with an open heart, humility, and hope, become the compass for connection and community transformation.

Before we turn the page – For as long as I can remember, I have been drawn to trees. As a child, I would sit in their shade, lean against their trunks, and gaze up in wonder. To me, they were majestic—the beauty marks of our landscape, the quiet givers of life. I imagined they held the many stories of all they had witnessed. As I grew older and began keeping a journal, my favorite place to think and write was under the sheltering arms of trees. Trees hold their history in their roots, much like we carry the wisdom of our ancestors within us. Just as each tree carries its own shape, texture, and character, so too do we. The exposed roots in the Benevolent Community graphic on the front cover are a reminder to stay grounded in goodness, generosity, and grace. The leaf and needle sketches scattered throughout this journal represent values essential to our integrity and humanity.

Reflection # 1

The oak tree has deep roots and wide branches, representing strength in connection and belonging. It is often seen as a symbol of endurance and resilience, much like the relationships we hope to build in a benevolent community.

"If we have no peace, it is because we have forgotten that we belong to each other."
– Mother Teresa

To Embrace Belonging – Rooted in Community

There is a quiet, often unseen labor in those who hold space for others, for truth, for possibility.

Their presence does not demand attention, yet it reshapes the room. It is in their listening, their restraint, their unwavering respect for the sacredness of each story that we begin to remember what it means to belong. This book begins here: with the honoring of that kind of presence. It begins in gratitude for those who dare to be fully human and who make it safe enough for others to do the same.

What follows are reflections rooted in this hope: that we might live with more care, more courage, and a deeper commitment to one another's dignity - and to the shared ground of our humanity.

"Belonging means more than having access; it means having a meaningful voice and the opportunity to participate in the design of political, social, and cultural structures. Belonging entails being respected at a basic level that includes the right to both contribute and make demands upon society and political institutions."
— john a. powell, Othering & Belonging Institute, UC Berkeley

"All real living is meeting."
— Martin Buber, I and Thou

Belonging

From the beginning of time to today, human beings have longed to belong -to one another and to something greater than self. This yearning is not merely emotional; it is elemental. It runs through our DNA, a deep and ancient understanding that to survive and to thrive - belonging is not optional. It is vital.

Belonging, in its truest form, is more than being included. As john a. powell reminds us, belonging is having the power to shape the space one belongs to. It is the right to be seen, heard, and valued in the design of community life. Belonging does not ask us to fit in; it calls us to co-create. This expansive view of belonging is one of the roots of benevolent communities.

Welcoming others into belonging is a first act of communal benevolence. It is how we say: You are not an outsider here. You are part of the story we are writing together. This invitation is not passive; it is an active practice of seeing one another fully and making room - room in our hearts, in our homes, in our civic structures. It is how a community begins to "come of age".

To gain a true sense of the depth of belonging, I have found that life requires us to first open ourselves to belonging

to life itself—to its seasons and cycles, its rhythms and
renewals. To behold the beauty and purpose of all living
things is to discover the interconnection of our ancestors,
our stories, and our breath.

Our human need to belong is not only an instinct for
survival but a call to honor the sacredness of being here -
on this planet, together with all people, creatures, plants,
water, wind, fire, and air. Belonging teaches us right from
wrong. It builds the foundation for empathy, compassion,
generosity, and integrity. None of this is fully known in
isolation. Where disconnection breeds mistrust and fear,
belonging nurtures relational trust and awakens our
understanding of shared humanity.

Even from birth, the instinct to belong is clear. One of a
newborn's first reflexes is to grasp a parent's finger—a
small physical gesture that reveals a profound truth: our
need to connect is as crucial as breath itself. Without
that rooted sense of connection, we have little reason
to grow into our fuller selves. Coming of age—
emotionally, ethically, spiritually—requires a sense of
belonging. It requires family, community, a circle of care
that says, "You matter. You are seen. You are ours."

Philosopher Martin Buber helps us understand this
even more deeply. In his teaching of I–Thou, he offers
that we do not become fully human in isolation, but in
relationship—when we meet one another not as objects
to be used (I–It), but as sacred beings to be encountered
(I–Thou). This kind of presence, this authentic seeing,
is the foundation of belonging. It is not merely
proximity—it is mutual recognition. In Buber's view,
belonging arises not from fitting in, but from being truly
met. When we open ourselves to see and be seen in this
way, community becomes not just a gathering of people,
but a sacred meeting ground of human dignity.

Belonging brings light to our hearts—even on a wet March Day.

 LORI ANN

This morning, I awoke to the distinct music of light and steady rain. A day some might call dreary - clouds hanging low, the sun shy and hidden. But through my window I see something else entirely. I see trees and shrubs welcoming the rain, their leaves smiling upward to catch and direct each drop, channeling water through stem and branch and trunk, ensuring that their roots receive the life-giving gift.

There's beauty budding too - leaves unfolding, flowers beginning to bloom, and birds visiting from near and far, perching on the limbs of the majestic oak tree that stands at the heart of our neighborhood. This 500+-year-old oak is more than a tree -it is a living witness, a keeper of time, and a symbol of communal belonging. Under its great canopy, I often pause and wonder: What has it seen? What storms have it withstood? What stories might it tell?

I am grateful to live in this small enclave of 26 families who share the responsibility of caring for this magnificent being. This shared caretaking is more than an agreement—it is an act of reciprocity. A reflection of what it means to belong to a place, to one another, and to something enduring. In tending to the tree, we tend to each other. And in doing so, we embody the quiet, steady truth: Belonging is not just a feeling. It is a way of being. It is where benevolence begins.

Essential Question:
What does true belonging mean to you—not just socially, but spiritually and relationally? How might you extend that sense of belonging to others in a way that honors both their voice and their presence?

Invitation to Practice:
Choose one relationship or shared space this week and practice Buber's I–Thou awareness. Greet someone not as a role or task but as a sacred being. Offer full presence. Observe how this changes your sense of belonging and connection, and their sense of being seen and heard.

Reflection #2

Aspen Trees do not stand alone, they grow in interconnected groves, sharing a single root system. This reflects how empathy binds us together, as we are all part of a larger whole.

"When we see another person fully and hold space for their story, we begin to remember what it means to be human."
- Parker J. Palmer

The Tapestry of Empathy – Seeing Ourselves In Others

I was ten years old when a chance meeting redirected my life. It shaped how I would think, listen, and move through the world in ways I'm still discovering.

One early spring afternoon, I was riding my bike through the woods—a typical ten-year-old's freedom ride in 1970. I followed my usual path: down into the gully, through the Sweetgums and Pines, to the small stream where I would stop and skip smooth stones.

But that day was different.

I smelled woodsmoke. Curious, I veered left, away from my familiar trail, guided only by my nose. Not far from the stream, I saw something unexpected: a man sitting beside a small fire. I stopped suddenly, straddling my bike.

He turned, looked at me gently, and said, "Hello." I felt like I had

startled a deer. Shame and curiosity twined in my chest. Yet in his eyes I saw a softness, and perhaps a shadow of sorrow.

He told me his name was Hank.

Still clutching the handlebars, I replied, "I'm Lori." I asked if he lived there, and many other questions that rose unfiltered in my coming-of-age mind. I had never met someone living outdoors before. I didn't yet know the term "homeless." Growing up in a suburb of Washington, D.C., this reality was not part of my world.

Hank was a war veteran, a storyteller, and someone deeply familiar with the forest. Over the weeks that followed, he became my first adult friend. He taught me about wilderness survival - and, in ways I'd only come to understand later, about people, grace, and life itself.

One day, I rode to visit and found his camp gone. A hollow sadness settled over me. I sat beside the firepit where we'd shared dandelion tea and noticed something under a stone - a piece of newsprint folded and smudged, my name on it.

It was a note from Hank.

Dear Lori,

I am sorry not to be here to say goodbye. I've never been good with farewells. I don't want you to worry or be sad.

Thank you—for so many things. First, for not being afraid of me. You treated me as family. I felt my dignity return. You listened to my stories and made me feel I had something to offer. You created a safe space for me to simply be.

Who would have thought such a gift would come from a little girl? You may be young, but you see with old soul eyes. I felt seen, heard, honored, and safe. I am so grateful.

You've given me the courage to try again—with my own family. So I'm going home. Maybe this time, they will see me as you did.

May you always shine,
Hank

I sat there for a long while, tears falling without warning - sad, happy, and confused all at once. I read his note again and again. The words that stayed with me then, and still: *dignity* and *create safe space.*

Something sacred shifted in me that day.

Rabbi Abraham Joshua Heschel once said, "In every event, something sacred is at stake." I believe that with my whole being. That spring, something holy moved through a small girl and a solitary man beside a fire in the woods.

We often imagine transformation as thunderous - a blinding flash, a grand epiphany. But sometimes, it's a quiet ember that burns for decades, illuminating the way we see, the way we feel, the way we choose to live.

Hank awakened my heart.

The Sufi poet Hafiz wrote, *"An awake heart is like a sky that pours light."* Hank opened that sky for me. I don't know where he is now, or if he still walks this earth. But he's never left me. He continues to be my light.

That meeting, that friendship, shifted my way of being. Hank's presence shaped how I listen, how I respond, how I hold others' questions and pain. Those early conversations echo through my work today - as a retreat facilitator, leadership coach, educator, and human advocate.

Through Hank, I began to wonder: *What would it mean to create safe space - not just between two people - but in entire communities?*

ROOTED IN HUMANITY Reclaiming Benevolence in Support of a Community's Coming of Age

Three roots of understanding began to take hold in me that spring:

1. We are born into our first learning environment. This setting, chosen for us, not by us - becomes the earliest root of how we understand the world. It forms the soil of our first stories.
2. Human experience is the root of knowing. We must travel the long road inward to know ourselves, and then outward, to truly know and empathize with another.
3. Safe space is essential. It is the root system that nourishes our physical, emotional, relational, and spiritual lives. We must do more than notice its absence - we must cultivate its presence.

These roots inspired me to launch *Create Safe Space, Inc.*, a Human-Centered nonprofit dedicated to building communities where awareness, dignity, and mutual respect are foundational. Our work weaves together character development, human centered skills, and mindful practices— the cornerstones of safe and benevolent community.

The value of safe space is not a new revelation. It is as old as humanity itself - carried in the wisdom of sages, educators, and seekers throughout time. But it must be remembered and returned to, seeded and cultivated in every life and generation.

Wherever Hank is, I hope he knows he has changed my life. Our meeting was sacred. It opened me to connection, to dignity, to civic care - and most of all, to empathy.

He saw me. And I saw him. And for a moment, we knew what it meant to simply be human - together.

Essential Question:
When have you truly seen yourself in another person's story, and how did that moment shape your understanding of empathy?

Invitation to Practice:
This week, create safe space for someone to share their story— without judgment, advice, or interruption. Simply listen. Notice what shifts in you when you hold another's humanity with gentle attention.

Reflection #3

The Willow is known for its resilience and stability to bend without breaking, much like the power of compassion, which like the fibrous roots of the willow, is the connective tissue that allows us to meet others with   grace and understanding.

"Prejudice is a burden that confuses the past, threatens the future, and renders the present inaccessible."

- Maya Angelou

The Courage to Care — Compassion, The Connective Tissue to Humanity

Compassion—
derived from The Latin compati, meaning to "suffer with" - asks something deep of us. It invites us not just to witness the pain of another, but to sit beside it, to lean toward it with tenderness, humility, and presence. Compassion is not pity from a distance; it is a courageous act of closeness. In a world often numbed by overwhelm or separation, choosing to care with compassion becomes an integral stance - one that opens a door to our shared humanity. This personal reflection explores how compassion, practiced as both feeling and action, becomes a foundation for benevolent communities where empathy guides connection, and where the courage to care has the power to transform isolation into belonging.

Introduction to Dr. Marlene Saunders Reflection

It is with deep respect and gratitude that I introduce the following guest reflection by Dr. Marlene A. Saunders, a valued member of our inaugural Benevolent Community Circle. In the spirit of compati—to suffer with—Dr. Saunders offers a deeply personal and prophetic meditation on compassion as both legacy and lifework.

Her words embody the truth that caring for others, especially in times of hardship and injustice requires immense courage. Through her lived experience and moral clarity, she reminds us that compassion is not a soft virtue, but a vital, steady force—a foundation upon which benevolent community can take root and thrive. Dr. Saunders has had a celebrated professional career in Social Work and is a committed community advocate. She was a longtime faculty member of her alma mater, Delaware State University, received her doctorate from the University of Pennsylvania, and now serves on the DSU Board of Trustees, having been appointed for a six-year term by Governor Carney. Dr. Saunders is a resident of Bridgeville, DE where she served as a Town Commissioner.

Judging People by the Color of Their Skin Prevents the Development of a Benevolent Community

By Dr. Marlene A. Saunders

A Social Context for Not Judging People by the Color of Their Skin

I often share with both Black and White people the ways race has shaped my life and the lives of African Americans across four centuries - since the beginning of enslavement in 17th-century America.

I sometimes refer to myself as a "Brown v. Board of Education child." In 1954, at age nine, I was one of a small group of Negro children who desegregated schools in New Castle, Delaware. I livedin Eden Park, a community outside Wilmington that had become predominantly Black. Still, a few white families remained - those who had not yet joined the wave of white flight.

Our household was multigenerational: my mother (Mom), my sister, my oldest brother Jimmy, my grandmother (Nana), and my step-grandfather (Pop Pop). My youngest brother was just eight months old when, in 1953, Mom contracted polio at the age of twenty-six and became paralyzed.

Uncle Billy, Nana, and Mom pooled their resources to purchase our home - a deed that still carried a race-restrictive covenant.

Though such clauses were declared unenforceable by 1948 and outlawed by the Fair Housing Act of 1968, they were still a common reality. Buying a home together was part of my family's plan to reunite and care for Mom. Nana became her primary caregiver, and the home provided the in-house support we all hoped she would receive.

Despite her disability, Mom remained active and determined. She helped run one of Daddy's stores, supported our academic pursuits - hiring tutors, advocating for our college admissions, and even opening a ceramics studio and school in our home with state support. Her tenacity extended to her identity: she was a proud race woman, deeply rooted in her African heritage. As we grew older, she became more candid about her views, often saying, "White people are the natural enemy of Black people. They are who they are, and they can't help it." These were not uncommon sentiments in the Black communities of both the North and South. Her guidance shaped how I approached white people for much of my life.

There Was No Reason to Be Prejudiced Against White People

When I started school in 1954, I was excited - despite often being labeled a slow learner. Back-to-school season was as thrilling as Christmas. Daddy always bought us new clothes, shoes, and school supplies, and I could barely sleep the night before.

That excitement vanished on the bus ride to school. White children from neighboring communities called us "coons," "ni**ers," "monkeys," and worse. They mocked and threatened us, pretending to spit, asking to see our palms to prove we were "almost white." My little brother Jimmy was terrified. I shielded him with my arm, holding him close.

Eventually, the harassment grew so severe that Mom called the school. The principal rode the bus for a few weeks, and the abuse ceased. Years later, during a Brown v. Board of Education recognition event at Delaware State University, Mom reflected, "If I had known then what I know now, I would've found a way to send my children to a school in Wilmington."

At school, bullying was less overt - but not absent. One white girl, Jean, unexpectedly became my protector. With her jet-black DA-style hair and black leather motorcycle jacket, I assumed she would be one of my tormentors. But whenever other white students taunted me, Jean would silently intervene, and they would stop. We never spoke - our only shared class was gym - but there was an unspoken connection. I even once tried to protect her when I feared she might hurt herself during a gymnastic vault.

"It Takes a Village to Raise a Child"

The behavior I witnessed from white students shocked me.

31

It was so unlike anything I had seen in my own community. We were taught to behave with dignity and respect. I wondered how these children, often poorly dressed and unclean, could believe they were superior to us. In our community, they were sometimes referred to as "poor white trash."

The Black communities I grew up in - Bridgeville, East Side Wilmington, Eden Park, and Prices Run - were true villages. They embodied the spirit of the African proverb: "It takes a village to raise a child." These were communities bound by love, collective responsibility, and economic interdependence.

Our segregated communities protected and nurtured us. Parents, grandparents, aunts, uncles, teachers, neighbors, and the Black church formed a network of care. Unlike white teachers who might have dismissed me as a slow learner, Black educators believed every child could learn. Nana and Mom sought out tutors, worked with teachers, and discovered teaching methods that worked for me. In time, I succeeded.

Our neighborhoods were rich in culture and community. We were surrounded by role models - professionals, artists, and educators. We attended churches and community centers without the burden of racism. Even our social spaces -The Spot, Notty Pine, the Monday Club - offered refuge.

The Pathway to a Benevolent Community Is Through Relationships

If I could show you a photo of Jean, you'd understand why I had prejudged her. But she defied my expectations. As a child, I didn't yet have the ability to distinguish between "good" and "bad" white people. My mother's lessons about white oppression were understandable and, to an extent, true to our experiences. But they had become ingrained in a way that shaped my assumptions for decades.

It wasn't until 2021, when I joined the inaugural Benevolent Community Circle during COVID, that I began to reflect on Jean—and what she represented. The memory opened a door I hadn't known was closed.

Through honest dialogue in spaces like the Southern Delaware Alliance for Racial Justice and the Benevolent Community, I began to form sincere relationships with white individuals. These were not based on trauma-sharing or mutual pity, but on authenticity, respect, and vulnerability. I knew it might be hard for some white participants to hear my raw truth - but I shared it anyway. And they stayed. They listened with compassion and sat in discomfort.

We grew in relationship - not just through dialogue, but through gathering. We broke bread, shared meals, sang to Motown. They came to my home for crab feasts and cookouts, and I to theirs.

I won't pretend all my prejudices have vanished. The political climate today is unsettling and regressive - especially for Black people. The threat to democratic ideals is real. Still, I know I have changed.

And so I say: thank you, Jean.

Essential Question:

What assumptions have I made about others based on their race, background, or appearance—and what relationships or stories might challenge those assumptions?

Invitation to Practice:

Take one meaningful step this month to deepen a relationship across racial or cultural lines—through shared conversation, a meal, or mutual storytelling. Listen fully, with openness, and without defense.

Reflection 4

The Cedar Tree has been loved across cultures for its strength, integrity, and ability to protect. It is often associated with wisdom and standing firm in one's beliefs.

"Without truth, there can be no trust, and without trust, no society can stand."
- Rabbi Jonathan Sacks, To Heal A Fractured World

The Art of Integrity – Trustworthy Actions for a Better Tomorrow

There are few places that, from the very first step out of a car, take my breath away - and in the same moment, breathe life into me. The small town of Blue Hill, Maine, was one such place. It filled my spirit with joy and an unshakable sense of belonging.

The purity of the light as it danced across the water, the wild bayberry bushes, and the worldliness of the tall spruce trees filled the air with the scent of history and memory. The reversing falls of Saltwater Pond flowed with a quiet wisdom, and the loon's beautiful, haunting calls stirred something sacred within me. It was as if the land itself whispered, "Welcome home."

It was here, in this serene corner of the world, that I first witnessed what I now understand as a benevolent community. Like most small rural towns, Blue Hill had

its differences—the lobstermen, the artists, the business owners, and the writers could be known to squabble now and then. But underneath it all was something rare and meaningful: a shared ethic of generous hearts, intellectual humility, honest work, pride in craftsmanship, and a deeply rooted concern for protecting the land and looking after one another.

It was also here that I met Howard and his remarkable family. Howard and his wife, Judith, had raised their children in a lovely timeworn farmhouse nestled between the bay and the pond. Now, a "pond" in Maine is often what others might call a lake—this one, fed by the bay's saltwater tides, was a living ecosystem filled with oysters, starfish, sea lions, eagles, loons, and kayakers who paddled through its calm, reflective surface.

And it was here, on a quiet road called Huckleberry Lane—named by Howard and Judith's children—that Howard sold my family four wooded acres of spruce forest.

When the time came to build a house, I brought Howard a sketch of my dream home, pieced together over the years in notebooks and wish-books, filled with clippings and ideas about what a Maine lake house might look like. I knew Howard did some sort of construction work, but he was humble -never boastful - and it wasn't until I asked that he revealed the full extent of his craftsmanship.

To my delight, Howard said he'd be happy to build the house and invited me to see several homes he and his team had constructed over the years. Each one felt like a work of art—thoughtfully designed, carefully built, full of heart and intention. I knew instantly that he and his team were the ones I could trust with this deeply personal project.

"There's only one thing," Howard said with quiet conviction. "I don't work with contracts. I only build one

house a year—for someone I trust. And we do it with a handshake."

You may be thinking, That's crazy! But that's only because you don't know Howard - his integrity, or the culture of a small town where one's good name truly matters. Where your word still means something. And so, we shook hands.

Nine months later, I moved into the most beautiful, soul-filled home I could have imagined. Not only was I surrounded by nature's wonders, the tides, the trees, the loons—but also by caring, thoughtful, and quite extraordinary neighbors. It was not to be my forever place, as life had other plans. But my time in Blue Hill remains a chapter of cherished memories and lessons - lessons that continue to shape how I see the world and how I choose to live in it.

It was in Blue Hill that I came to believe, more deeply than ever, that benevolence, trustworthiness, and integrity are not relics of a bygone era. They are very much alive. They exist - and if they exist in one place, they can be nurtured and created in another.

Each day, we are witness to so much - interactions, transactions, conversations, silences. Ordinary moments and extraordinary ones. But I've come to learn that being a witness is only the beginning. What we choose to embrace from what we witness is what matters most.

Blue Hill was more than a beautiful place. It was a lived-reminder that trustworthy actions, rooted in shared values, still exist. That integrity is not just about honesty - it is about alignment between our values and our actions. And it is this alignment that builds the kind of community that can carry us into a better tomorrow.

The art of integrity is not a grand gesture—it is a thousand small decisions. A handshake that holds. A home that's built with care. A neighbor who listens. A choice to

act in alignment with the world we wish to build.

Because the art of integrity is not found only in extraordinary people, but in ordinary choices made with care and consistency. It lives in the heart of a community that honors its word, protects what is sacred, and shows up with fidelity to one another and to the earth we share. This is how integrity becomes a light - shining forward as a way to inspire and build a better tomorrow.

Essential Question:

When have I experienced or witnessed an act of integrity that left a lasting impression—and how might I embody that same spirit in my own choices and relationships?

Invitation To Practice:

Identify one relationship, project, or community space in your life where trust and integrity are needed. Commit to one small action this week that demonstrates consistency between your values and your actions—whether *it's a promise kept, a truth gently told, or a responsibility embraced with care.*

Reflection #5

The Apple Tree is a symbol of Generosity and Abundance. It continuously provides fruit, symbolizing giving freely and abundantly without expectation.

"No one has ever become poor by giving."
-Anne Frank
"All flourishing is mutual. The moral covenant of reciprocity calls us to honor our responsibilities for all we have been given, for all that we have taken. It's our turn now, long overdue."
-Robin Wall Kimmerer, from Braiding Sweetgrass

Generosity Within Us: A Human Response to The Paradox of Good and Evil

I have always wondered, "Why, in a world filled with beauty and bounty, does evil and scarcity exist?"

This question has echoed through my life, not just as a philosophical musing, but as a lens through which I've studied history- not solely to understand civilizations, but to more deeply grasp the human experience. What causes one to destroy, while another chooses to uplift? What motivates one to be generous of heart, and another to allow the fear of scarcity to scar their spirit?

How do ideologies grow that center on harm, when the potential for loving-kindness exists in equal measure? It seems to me that evil works off a model of scarcity. A

belief that "I need what you have, and I cannot be whole without it."

Whatever the "it" may be - land, power, money, fame- this hunger is not rooted in the very human frailties and failings of need, but in fear and control.

From this lens, I have come to see the opposite of evil not merely as "goodness," but as generosity through benevolence - an ethic of abundance, of freely giving and extending oneself to others, not because we must, but because we can.

To be benevolent is to choose a path that affirms life, community, and the worthiness of every human being. It is to live not by taking, but by giving. To resist the seduction of scarcity and stand instead in the light of shared possibility.

Of course, this is an altruistic path. One where generosity is not simply charity, but a practice of empathy, rooted in the belief that we belong to one another.

Evil and generosity exist in tension. One seeks to diminish life, the other to elevate it.

There have always been polarizing ideas - those that compete with the righteousness of our humanity. I have long wondered about the strange infatuation some people have with evil: its vow of immortality, its illusion of glory, its seductive promises. And yet, the enduring cost is almost always destruction, hopelessness, and grief.

This rivalry between evil and good has found its way into every form of expression - music, philosophy, and literature. Consider the opera Faust, the masterpiece St. Michael Vanquishing Satan by Raphael, and the many literary works that give voice to this eternal tension: Paradise Lost by John Milton, Lord of the Flies by

William Golding, To Kill a Mockingbird by Harper Lee, The Picture of Dorian Gray by Oscar Wilde, and Beloved by Toni Morrison.

Through each of these stories, we see the consequences of evil and the moral courage required to resist it. We see how the seeds of fear and hatred, once planted, can overtake a landscape—and how only a more powerful force like love, integrity, or generosity can truly dismantle its hold.

I am persuaded that war, in its most tragic form, is the ultimate manifestation of evil's reach. It is not just violence, but the strategic and intentional elimination of another's existence or identity in the name of power. It is of importance to realize that evil begs for a response, and acts of evil require us to defend good – life itself. Yet, even when wars "end," they often leave behind a more silent kind of brutality - what I have come to understand as "silent wars": the simmering resentments, hatreds, and biases that linger beneath the surface. And sadly, the paradox of war is often found in the tug of war between wanting to live in peace – and wanting to fill a need either by exploiting what another can provide for you or with what another has.

Silent wars are found in the ongoing racial prejudices toward African Americans before and after the Civil War… the persistence of antisemitism long after the Holocaust… the discrimination of indigenous people, refugees, and the displaced… These are the silent wars. Wars against human thriving. Wars against the right to belong, to be safe, to be free, to live together in peace.

And these wars are not waged by weapons alone - they are sustained by narratives. Narratives of "otherness," superiority, entitlement, and fear.

In the face of these narratives, benevolence becomes more than a kindness - it becomes a form of protection.

To live generously, in a world trained to measure value through accumulation is evolutionary.

To choose community over conquest, empathy over envy, and service over self-interest is to say: "I believe in a humanity that honors life's purpose over power."

I've often returned to language to help name and distinguish the paths we walk.

Consider the roots and companions of these two opposing forces:

Evil – from Old English yfel – speaks to profound immorality. It is often characterized not just by harmful actions, but by ideologies that deny the humanity of others.

Companion Words: Anathema, Decay, Sinful, Depravity, Corruption, Wickedness.

Benevolence – from the Latin bene, "to wish well." It is a disposition of goodwill and a readiness to help others— not because one must, but because one chooses to.

Companion Words: Kindness, Generosity, Blessing, Empathy, Mercy, Service, Community.

We live in a time that desperately needs benevolence in action. A University of Florida Research Team led by Shawn Burke (2007), found that when assessing trust, people often look for three things: "ability, integrity, and benevolence."

Without benevolence, integrity has no empathy, and ability becomes mechanical. With benevolence, both are humanized. It is within our humanity that generosity lives.

So, what does generosity look like in practice?

It looks like a neighbor who delivers food without being asked. A teacher who refuses to give up on a struggling

student. A person who listens without judgment. A stranger who steps in when someone is being mistreated. A community that shares its resources so that no one is left behind.

Generosity is not only in what we give - it is *in how we give*.

Freely.

Willingly.

Without expectation of return.

And it is also in what we refuse to manifest and take.

We refuse to manifest fear, hate, and evil intent.

We refuse to take someone's dignity, safety, or belonging in the name of our own comfort.

To live generously is to embody benevolence to become, in practice, the opposite of evil.

We must begin to see generosity not as a soft virtue, but as a moral stance. A defiant act in a world that often rewards selfishness and scarcity.

I believe that to build communities truly worthy of our humanity, we must practice generosity as a collective ethic. We must shift from asking "What is mine?" to "What can I share?"

From "What can I control?" to "What can I contribute?"

Because in the end, the legacy of a person, a community, or a nation will not be found in what they took- but in what they gave. And how that giving sustained life, nurtured trust, and preserved the sacred possibility of peace.

Essential Question:

Where in your life or community have you seen generosity change a relationship, restore trust, or repair harm? How might you grow your own practice of benevolence in response to the needs you see?

Invitation to Practice:

This week, identify one act of generosity you can offer with no expectation of return. It may be time, attention, resources, or a simple gesture of care. Make it intentional. Make it relational. Make it part of your way of being in the world.

Reflection 6:

The Sycamore symbolizes awakening, seeing anew, and spiritual transformation. Sycamores are trees of lifted sight — a reminder that sometimes we must climb above fear or assumption to witness what is truly before us.

"The face of the Other is the trace of the Infinite."
— Emmanuel Levinas, Totality and Infinity (1961)

"Twice the Stars" – A Vision for a More Expansive Humanity

At the intersection of benevolence and humanity, there exists a public square. It is not a place made of brick and mortar, nor one bound by geography. Rather, it is a meeting ground of the spirit, a space where we come together in our highest aspirations, where we extend our hands and hearts to one another, clothed in the finest garments of our shared humanity.

Philosopher Emmanuel Levinas offers a way of understanding this space. For him, ethics begins not in theory but in encounters. When we face another person, especially someone different, unfamiliar, or vulnerable - we are called not to define them, but to respond to them. In his words, *"the face of the Other is the trace of the Infinite."* This means that every face we meet carries with it a divine summons - not to power, but to responsibility.

To see another not as a category, but as a call. As a possibility. I often imagine myself standing in this square - in this sacred gathering space—where the air hums with the quiet murmur of kindness, and the very ground seems to pulse with integrity, generosity, creativity, empathy, and love. Here, there is no competition or scarcity, no fear of the stranger, no walls that divide. Instead, there is an unspoken understanding: that to be fully human is to wish one another well.

In the center of this square stands a statue of a two-headed calf. At first glance, it appears an oddity, something unexpected, unsettling even. Yet at its base is a poem by Laura Gilpin, offering a lens through which to see this creature in all its wonder:

"Tomorrow when the farm boys find this freak of nature, they will wrap his body in newspaper and carry him to the museum. But tonight, he is alive and in the north field with his mother. It is a perfect summer evening: the moon rising over the orchard, the wind in the grass. And as he stares into the sky, there are twice as many stars as usual."

This poem speaks to the essence of how we perceive the world and one another. It is an invitation to look beyond the surface of what we call normal and see the luminous, fleeting beauty in what we might otherwise dismiss.

The two-headed calf is a metaphor for our own duality, the tension between how we categorize difference and how we might instead embrace wonder. Too often, we are trained to sort the world into what is familiar and what is strange, what is acceptable and what is "other." We are conditioned to name, to label, to define. But wonder asks something different of us. Wonder is not about naming - it is about noticing with generosity of heart. It is about holding space for the mysteries that do not demand explanation.

If we listen carefully, the two-headed calf has much to teach us about how we see ourselves and others.

"Tomorrow, the farm boys will find the calf and wrap it in newspaper" preserving it as a curiosity, something to be studied, categorized, made sense of. This is the way much of the world operates: we contain what we do not understand. We make spectacles of difference rather than dwelling in its beauty.

"But tonight, in the quiet of the north field, the calf is alive. It stands beside its mother, bathed in moonlight, the wind whispering through the grass. In this moment, the world is not focused on its difference but on its presence. It sees the night sky not as one-headed creatures do, but with twice the wonder. There are twice as many stars."

This is the invitation the poem extends: to see the world through the eyes of awe rather than judgment. To recognize that what makes us different can also make us more expansive. To understand that the most profound shifts in human perception do not come from categorization but from connection.

Levinas might say that in this moment of beholding—not explaining—we begin to understand our humanity. The "face of the Other" is not just something we notice; it is something that changes us. It reminds us that to be human is to be responsible for the humanity of others.

Benevolence as a Way of Seeing

What if, instead of rushing to label, we allowed benevolence to guide our vision? What if we approached one another not with the instinct to assess, but with the impulse to honor?

Benevolence is not merely kindness—it is a way of being in the world that extends beyond mere goodwill. It is a practice of seeing. To be benevolent is to offer the best of ourselves not because it is deserved, but because it is needed. It is to recognize that the core of our humanity is not measured by how we categorize one another, but by how we care for one another.

If the public square is where we meet, then benevolence is the foundation upon which it stands. It is what transforms an ordinary space into a sanctuary of belonging. It is what allows us to step beyond our conditioned responses and see with fresh eyes. It is the force that transforms a "freak of nature" into a being bathed in moonlight, capable of seeing twice the stars.

A World Reimagined

Imagine, for a moment, a world that fully embraces the lesson of the two-headed calf. A world where we do not discard or otherize what we do not understand, but instead draw closer to it with curiosity and care.

What would it look like to build our communities not around exclusion but around wonder? Not around fear of difference, but around the richness it brings? What if we saw in one another the possibility of twice as many stars?

This is not a utopian dream. It is the work of the benevolent heart—of a benevolent community. It is the practice of choosing to see with generosity, to listen with humility, to extend ourselves beyond the boundaries we have been given.

To stand in the public square of our shared humanity is to acknowledge that we are all, in some way, the two-headed calf—unusual, wondrous, worthy of belonging. And if we are to build a world that truly reflects our

highest aspirations, then we must be willing to stand together, under the rising moon, seeing one another fully, and holding open the space for twice as much light.

Essential Question:

Where in your life have you met difference with fear or confusion—and what might it look like to meet it instead with wonder, responsibility, or care?

Practice Invitation:

Choose one encounter this week—a conversation, a disagreement, a surprising difference—and pause before reacting. Look again with the eyes of benevolence. What "twice as many stars" might be revealed when you choose to see rather than assess?

Reflection 7:

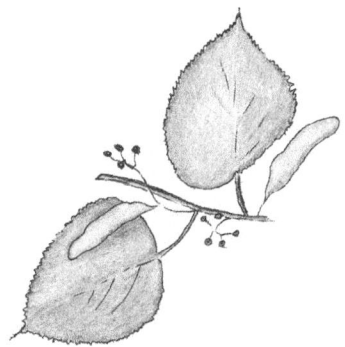

The Linden Tree is also known as the Tree of Community. it symbolizes collective well-being, protection, and public gathering. Traditionally, Linden Trees were planted at the center of villages where people gathered to hold council. It symbolizes care for the common good and was often called the "tree of friendship."

"The best way to find yourself is to lose yourself in the service of others." – Mahatma Gandhi

Lighting the Way – Service as a Path to Civic Health

"Service Begins With Listening.
Listening builds trust.
And trust creates the conditions for collective action that strengthens the civic health of our communities."
-Joseph Lawson

Introduction to Joseph Lawson's Reflection:

In our exploration of what sustains thriving communities, we turn to the concept of civic health — a measure not only of institutional vitality, but of the spirit of care that pulses through our neighborhoods. Civic health reveals itself in small acts of compassion, in the willingness of individuals to serve their neighbors, and in community members joining hands to meet shared challenges. It's more than civic engagement—it is the benevolent energy that

animates our collective well-being and reflects the depth of connection and concern we hold for one another.

The New Hampshire Civic Health Index (2020), defined civic health as "the ways in which residents of a community (or state) participate in activities that strengthen well-being, enhance interconnections, build trust, help each other, talk about public issues and challenges, volunteer in government and nonprofit organizations, stay informed, and participate directly in crafting solutions to various social and economic challenges."

It is with this in mind, and much joy that I introduce this chapter's contributor, Joseph Lawson. Joe's wisdom and leadership have profoundly shaped my understanding of how service can nurture the civic health of a community. Joe is a dear friend, colleague, and a member of the inaugural Benevolent Community Initiative Circle. His commitment to listening, collaboration, and action reflects the very heart of what it means to build a benevolent community.

Joseph Lawson, is a Sussex County, DE resident and longtime SDARJ board member (2020 - 2025), who brings decades of corporate and nonprofit leadership experience. A graduate of Yale University (B.A. in African American Studies) and Columbia University (MBA in Marketing), he has held leadership roles at Verizon, Comcast, ESPN, and Black Entertainment Television, always with a focus on promoting diversity in content and leadership.

I also wish to express my gratitude to Charlotte King, founder of the Southern Delaware Alliance for Racial Justice (SDARJ). During my years in Delaware, I actively participated in SDARJ, co-facilitating their Dialogue Toward Ending Racism program and helping plan various events. When I began developing the Benevolent Community Initiative, Charlotte was the first to support my

efforts. From her passion and persistence, I learned that service, when rooted in deep concern for the community, can genuinely strengthen its well-being.

A Brief History of SDARJ

In the spring of 2015, a group of Sussex County residents organized a study group to read and discuss *The New Jim Crow: Mass Incarceration in the Age of Colorblindness* by Michelle Alexander. Moved by similar initiatives nationwide and deeply concerned about the disproportionate targeting and punishment of African American men in the criminal justice system, Charlotte F. King and Jo Klinge founded the Southern Delaware Alliance for Racial Justice in June 2015.

Since then, SDARJ has developed programs, dialogue groups, and town halls that have educated, inspired, and engaged those living and working in Southern Delaware— building relationships across differences and working to end the corrosive racism that divides communities.

Lighting the Way: Service as a Path to Community Civic Health By Josheph Lawson

When we hear the word "service," a cascade of meanings may come to mind—each shaped by our personal experiences and the context in which the word is used. It is a chameleon of a term: sometimes transactional, sometimes deeply personal, sometimes sacred.

The first fundamental of serving is listening. Whether a waiter asks for your dinner order or a customer service representative inquires about your problem, true service cannot occur without genuine listening. Listening with a benevolent ear enhances the quality of service offered. How well -and how consistently - you listen can be a truer indicator of whether you care, more so than anything you

could say. You can claim to care, but words alone convey less power than the act of listening.

In unhealthy societies and relationships, flawed listening leads to poor service, fractured relationships, and negative outcomes. One could argue that the suspicion, polarization, and dysfunction we see in society today stem from an epidemic of not listening. We are failing to truly hear one another, and as a result, we are failing to truly serve each other.

To help transform a community, anyone seeking to create real change must prioritize listening -deeply, intentionally, and without an agenda. Then, ask good questions - questions that:

- Demonstrate that you have been listening, as they are based on what you heard.
- Show you care about what was shared.
- Seek clarification rather than rushing to assert your opinion (unless invited).

Questions are among the most powerful tools in human experience. Being skilled at asking questions is the hallmark of a great organizer. While many can deliver an inspiring speech or sermon, far fewer can make others feel truly listened to and heard.

Effective questions, paired with attentive listening, produce three crucial outcomes:

1. Information needed to solve problems.
2. Trust between the speaker and the listener.
3. A sense of being acknowledged and valued.

When we listen well and ask thoughtful questions, our service becomes more effective - and is more likely to be perceived as valuable.

A Story of Listening and Service

When I took on the role of Executive Director of the Southern Delaware Alliance for Racial Justice, one of our goals was to build a coalition of local social change organizations united for community improvement and fairness.

On June 27th -just three weeks before the anniversary of Civil Rights icon John Lewis's passing - several organizations approached me to ask if SDARJ had anything planned for the anniversary. More than 1,600 "Good Trouble Lives On" events were scheduled nationwide, but none in southern Delaware.

Though we hadn't planned anything, hearing the request compels us to organize an event despite having no venue, budget, agenda, or speakers. We reached out to local organizations to become promotional partners, and within days, ten had joined us. By July 7th, just ten days before the anniversary, we secured a permit for Johnny Walker Beach—the only beach in the area historically open to Black visitors during segregation.

Our partners sent out coordinated announcements, and soon registration filled to capacity. On the day of the event, a dangerous heat advisory was issued. One of our partner pastors graciously offered to host the event in her church. With just four and a half hours' notice, our network spread the word about the venue change.

We feared turnout would be small - yet people continued to arrive until the sanctuary overflowed into standing room only. The energy was electric. Powerful speakers delivered their messages, leading to at least three standing ovations. This became the largest non-entertainment event our organization had ever hosted.

Why? Because we listened. We responded to what the community said it wanted. Because of the relationships and trust we had built over time, people showed up - not just for the event but for one another.

The result was more than a successful gathering; it was a spark. The event strengthened trust, built new lines of communication, and laid the groundwork for ongoing collaboration among progressive organizations in our area.

As Deepak Iyer poignantly states, "Service, I've learned, is as much about how we show up in the world as it is about what we do. It's in the way we greet a stranger, hold space for someone's story, or infuse gratitude into the mundane."

This resonates deeply with our theme. The quality of our listening defines how we show up in our communities, linking our civic service to the health of our civic life.

Essential Question:

How might listening more deeply to our neighbors transform the way we serve - and the way our communities thrive?

Invitation to Practice:

In the coming week, identify one conversation in which you will practice intentional listening. Focus entirely on understanding the other person's perspective before offering your thoughts.
Afterward, reflect: What did I learn? How did listening in this way shift the relationship? How might I build on this trust in service of the community?

Reflection 8:

The Banyan Tree, a symbol of Interconnectedness, Shelter, and Inclusion. The Banyan Tree spreads wide, creating a canopy under which many can gather. It represents acceptance, creating space for all, and the interconnected nature of life.

"We are in an imagination battle...and the future will be shaped by who is willing to imagine together, who is brave enough to weave together the future we long for." - **adrienne maree brown**

Weaving the Whole: Rooted in the Wisdom of Many - Becoming One Community

Cultural Organizing: A Path to Benevolent Community

The soul of a benevolent community comes from its understanding of cultural organizing. It is not merely an academic concept or a theoretical framework—it is a way of seeing, a way of being, a way of making sense of the world. It is how we engage with and honor the cultures that shape us, and in turn, shape our communities.

Culture is formed through experience, through faith, traditions, and rituals. It is shaped by what we see and hear, the music that moves us, the stories that inspire

us, the food that nourishes us, and the art that stirs something deep within. Every individual carries a unique cultural imprint, a lens through which they interpret the world. These interpretations, rooted in lived experiences, give meaning to life, shaping identities and connections. Cultural organizing is the intentional act of bringing these perspectives together—not to merge them into one indistinct whole, but to arrange them in a way that allows them to be seen, understood, and celebrated for what they are.

From childhood, we are taught to sort—to recognize patterns, to categorize, to make sense of the world through structure. We group colors, shapes, and numbers. We piece together puzzles. We learn to differentiate between what is familiar and what is unfamiliar.
This act of sorting does not stop at objects; it extends to people, communities, and ideas. Cultural organizing builds upon this instinct not to separate, but to bring order to the beautiful complexity of human diversity. It is about creating a framework that allows cultures to coexist in ways that enrich rather than erase.

In my work, I see culture as a living landscape, shaped by time, ancestry, and collective memory. Every person carries a story of how they have been impacted by the past, by the people who came before them, by the traditions that have been passed down. Some of these stories are deeply personal, while others are collective, held within families, communities, or entire nations. When I engage in cultural organizing, I am not merely collecting stories; I am mapping them—understanding what people hold dear, what gives them a sense of belonging. This process allows me to see culture not as a static entity but as a dynamic, evolving force.

For too long, society has operated under the idea of the "melting pot," a notion that different cultures should

blend into one homogeneous identity. But cultural
organizing challenges this perspective. It does not seek
to dissolve differences but to highlight them, to create a
framework where every culture retains its distinctiveness
while existing harmoniously within the whole. This shift in
perspective moves us from assimilation to acceptance, from
erasure to celebration. It allows us to see that the strength
of a community lies not in its uniformity but in its
diversity.

Cultural theorist Raymond Williams defined culture as
"a whole way of life." He argued that culture is not just a
collection of customs or artistic expressions, but the living,
breathing fabric of a community—its values, relationships,
language, rituals, and shared meanings. To accept cultural
differences, then, is to welcome new ways of being human
into our shared life. It is to expand the space in which life
can be lived with dignity, imagination, and integrity.

When we share our traditions, faiths, rituals, foodways,
art, and cultural wisdom, we weave an abundant basket
of human knowledge—one that carries the strength of
many hands and the nourishment of many stories. This
collective sharing does not dilute identity; it deepens
connection. It teaches us that acceptance is not passive
tolerance - it is an active embrace. And it grounds
community in something far more resilient than
uniformity: a shared understanding that difference is not
a threat, but a gift.

Once we embrace the idea of cultural organizing, we
begin to see how it transforms our relationships, our
communities, and our way of thinking. It teaches us to
move away from criticism and into curiosity, to replace
judgment with wonder. Instead of viewing differences
as barriers, we start to see them as doorways—openings
into new ways of understanding, new ways of being. A
benevolent community is built upon this foundation. It

is a space where cultures do not compete but contribute, where learning from one another is not an obligation but a joy.

A community that engages in cultural organizing uplifts empathy, compassion, and beauty. It fosters generosity—not just in the material sense, but in the way we share space, stories, and perspectives. It cultivates dignity by allowing people to be seen and valued for who they are. It encourages a generosity of spirit, a willingness to listen, to engage, to honor what others bring to the table. Cultural organizing is not just about structuring cultures—it is about making room for them to flourish.

In practice, cultural organizing requires intentionality. It requires listening—truly listening—to the experiences of others. It demands a willingness to question our assumptions, to let go of rigid ideas about what culture should be, and instead embrace what culture already is. It asks us to recognize our own biases and to open ourselves to perspectives that challenge us. It calls for action—not just passive acknowledgment, but active participation in creating spaces that are inclusive and affirming.

The impact of cultural organizing extends beyond individuals; it shapes institutions, policies, and systems. It influences the way schools educate, the way workplaces foster inclusivity, the way governments create policies that serve diverse communities. It shifts narratives in media, in literature, in the arts. It redefines what it means to belong. When cultural organizing becomes a guiding principle, it creates ripples that extend far beyond the immediate community—it becomes a movement, a force for change.

At its core, cultural organizing is about harmony. It does not seek to eliminate differences but to arrange them in a way that brings out their beauty. It is the art of making

space, the practice of honoring stories, the commitment
to building communities that thrive not in spite of their
differences, but because of them.

A benevolent community does not emerge by chance; it
is cultivated through intentional acts of understanding,
engagement, acceptance, and celebration. Cultural
organizing is the foundation upon which such
communities are built. It is the recognition that our
cultures—our stories, our traditions, our ways of seeing
the world—are not obstacles but gifts. It is a way of seeing
and being in harmony with our humanity.

Essential Question:
What aspect of your own cultural story—tradition, value,
or ritual—might you share with others to enrich collective
understanding?
What might you receive in return?

Invitation to Practice:
Host or attend a small gathering, perhaps a meal, a story
circle, or a seasonal ritual where different cultural
practices are honored and shared. Make room for listening
without comparison and celebrate what is offered with
curiosity and gratitude.

Reflection 9:

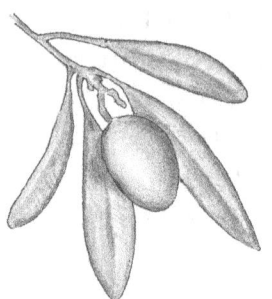

> The Olive Tree symbolizes peace, witness, reconciliation, and ancestral roots. It is an ancient tree, often growing for hundreds (even thousands) of years. It has stood through wars, droughts, and shifting empires. It is seen as a sacred tree in many faith traditions, often seen as a witness to history.

"We are not makers of history. We are made by history."
— Reverend Dr. Martin Luther King, Jr.

Witnessing History: An Ancestral Root for Benevolent Community

The work of building a Benevolent Community is fundamentally about forging trustworthy relationships, creating safe spaces through accessible and human-centered boundaries, and fostering deep, honest engagement. At its core, this process requires witnessing history - both personal and collective - as an integral step in a community's coming of age.

To witness history is to engage with the past not as a distant series of events, but as a living record of human experiences that continues to shape our present and inform our future. A mature community does not turn away from its history but instead leans into it, examining how past events have influenced individuals, families, and social structures. It seeks clarity that comes from shared reflection, courageous truth-telling, and the willingness to acknowledge both wounds and wisdom.

In this way, building a Benevolent Community is an active practice. It invites us to ask essential questions that reveal the soul of both individuals and the collective. It encourages us to pay attention to how we respond, choosing understanding over reactivity, reflection over defensiveness. This work is about more than dialogue; it is about developing the emotional, intellectual, and ethical maturity necessary for a community to truly "come of age."

Unearthing Wisdom: History as a Guide

If we think of history as an archaeological dig, then each layer we uncover offers us deeper insight - not only into past events but into the human responses to those events. It is not history's chronology that matters most, but rather the impact those moments had on people's lives and the lessons they offer for today.

To do this work well, we must turn to the truth-tellers, the elders, the historians, the witnesses who carry the weight of lived experience. These are the individuals who have cultivated a deep connection with their own inner teacher while also holding space for the broader historical narrative. Their stories, reflections, and insights are not just personal recollections; they are guideposts for collective learning, offering the wisdom necessary to nurture a better future - one that upholds the virtues of justice, compassion, and shared humanity.

The Interconnectedness of Our Humanity

A Benevolent Community does not exist in isolation; it is deeply aware of the interconnectedness of all human life. It recognizes that belonging is not about erasing individuality but about honoring it within the greater whole. Such a community understands that each of us bears responsibility - not only for preserving history but for shaping the trajectory of our shared future. At this critical intersection of community and humanity,

we stand together, aware that the choices we make
- whether to rise in collective wisdom or to falter in
division - will define the path ahead. We are part of a
spiral of history, one that can ascend toward healing
and understanding or descend into fragmentation and
neglect.

Reframing Our Understanding of History

History is often taught as a series of events, but at its
heart, history is the study of change over time - a record
of human responses to life's challenges and opportunities.
It is political, social, economic, cultural, and intellectual; it
is deeply personal and profoundly communal.

Too often, we examine isolated moments in history
without considering the broader trajectory - how
each event shapes what comes next, how ideas evolve,
and how societies develop intellectually, emotionally,
and spiritually. By shifting our perspective, we move
beyond seeing history as a fixed record and instead
engage with it as a living conversation—one that invites
us to be both learners and participants in shaping
what comes next.

A Benevolent Community is, at its essence, a clear-eyed
witness to history, a repository of collective wisdom
that is invaluable to any society seeking to build a more
just and compassionate future. To witness history is
to take responsibility for it, to learn from it, and to
use its lessons to forge new paths forward. In doing
so, we affirm our shared humanity and embrace the
responsibility of shaping a world worthy of future
generations.

Essential Question

What truths, those long hidden, half-remembered, or
newly uncovered - do you feel called to witness more
deeply? How might acknowledging these truths help you
or your community grow in wisdom, compassion, and
maturity?

Invitation to Practice

Find a place that invites quiet reflection—a local
monument, historical marker, elder's home, or the shade
of an olive tree. Bring a journal. As you sit, consider a
moment in history that lives within or around you. What
does it ask of you now? What might it mean to witness
with both memory and responsibility?

Reflection 10

The Baobab Tree is a symbol of wisdom, collective growth, and lifelong learning. It is known as the "Tree of Life," the Baobab holds water and nourishes the communities around it, representing endurance, and shared responsibility in creating a thriving community.

"We are each other's harvest; we are each other's business; we are each other's magnitude and bond."
- Gwendolyn Brooks

Final Words: A Community Coming of Age

There comes a moment in the life of every individual, and every community, when it becomes clear that the work of maturing is no longer optional. It is essential. It is time.

This book began with a simple but profound belief: that we are capable of building communities worthy of our shared humanity. Communities grounded not in transaction or tolerance, but in belonging, trust, compassion, generosity, empathy, integrity, and service. Communities that do not merely grow old, but come of age - with clarity of purpose, courage of voice, and care for one another.

Throughout these pages, we have explored what it means to live with benevolence at the center of our way of being. We have asked essential questions, held space for vulnerability, reflected on lived experiences, and honored the wisdom that emerges when people are invited to show up fully. Together, we have returned again

and again to the idea that a benevolent community is
not simply created, it is cultivated, with intention, with
imagination, and with love.

And now, in this final chapter, I offer my deepest gratitude
to the others who joined in this journey. Their voices,
stories, and insights are part of the very soil from which
this work has grown.

Natasha Warsaw's invitation to join her to hold space in
community during a time that we were isolated to our
own space, her generosity and openness to explore the
idea of building a path to benevolent community, and her
poignant words of Introduction to this book.

Dr. Marlene Saunders, whose essay on *Compassion*
reminded us that to care for others is not an abstraction,
but a daily act of presence and courage.

Joseph Lawson, who, in his reflection *Lighting the Way:
Service as a Path to Civic Health*, illuminates how acts of
volunteerism and service are not side notes to community
life—but vital practices of civic well-being and relational
integrity.

At the end of this final reflection, you will find other
voices of our first Benevolent Community Circle who
share their thoughts, testimonials, and a poem or two that
that together form a chorus. Each one a note in the song
of what it means to live with open hearts and outstretched
hands. These contributions are more than supportive;
they are *generative*. They speak to the kind of maturity
a community can grow into when we center dialogue,
honor each person's experience, and dare to live with
principled generosity.

In every circle, every conversation, every story shared, I
witnessed something sacred: a coming of age. Not one

marked by age or accomplishment, but by awareness. By the willingness to see another's truth and still say, "you belong."

This is the quiet miracle of benevolent community: it asks us not to agree on everything, but to stand together in the work of being human.

What emerges from such work is not perfection, but trust. Not certainty, but openness. Not a utopia, but a place where people feel seen, valued, and heard. It is in these very spaces -what we've called "safe enough" spaces - that transformation becomes possible. Where someone's story unlocks another's healing. Where a difficult question invites a shared insight. Where silence is honored, and listening is sacred.

When we intentionally cultivate these values - belonging, compassion, trustworthiness, generosity, empathy, integrity, and service - we begin to experience what it means to be part of something greater than ourselves. We begin to recognize that a healthy, thriving community is not the result of policies alone, but of practices. It is made, moment by moment, in how we treat one another, how we listen, how we respond, and how we hold space for what is still becoming.

This is how a community comes of age.

Not in grand declarations, but in the quiet acts of care.
Not in uniformity, but in curiosity and acceptance.
Not by erasing difference, but by weaving it into the whole.

This is the vision of a benevolent community rooted in humanity. It is not a distant dream. It is already within reach - whenever we choose to lead with heart, to listen with humility, and to act with integrity.

My hope is that this book leaves you with more than inspiration. I hope it leaves you with *questions that matter*, stories that linger, and practices that inspire. I hope it calls you to be part of this shared work - to nurture the places where you live and lead, to serve with purpose, and to build communities that are not only good to live in, but good to grow up in, grow old in, and grow wise within.

Together, we can raise communities that are ready-
Ready to serve,
Ready to listen,
Ready to love,
Ready to come of age.

Essential Question:

In what ways have you witnessed a community honor the dignity of its members — not just in moments of grief or celebration, but on ordinary days, through the steady, shared labor of showing up for one another?

Invitation to Practice:

A Circle of Acknowledgement

Gather in community and create space for naming and honoring the contributions, voices, and presence of others. Invite participants to speak aloud a moment when someone in the community acted with care, courage, or integrity, something that helped the whole grow stronger. Make it a ritual of recognition. Then close by reflecting together on this question: *What responsibility do we now hold to sustain this kind of care as we move forward together?*

 LORI ANN

Voices from our Benevolent Community Circle

*It is an honor to share a few more voices from our first
Benevolent Community Circle — reflections that carry the
spirit of our gathering, giving shape to the experiences and
insights that rose from our time together.*

Clint:

When I first discovered the retreat *A Path to Creating
Benevolent Community* on the Center for Courage &
Renewal website, I became intrigued and wonder what
exactly does that mean. I went to my dictionary and
looked up benevolent which I found defined as: showing
or motivated by sympathy and understanding and
generosity. I also saw that benevolent originated from
Latin bene volent- 'well wishing'.

As I looked further at the invitation, I discovered the
facilitators were offering to lead this retreat of yearlong
monthly conversations for no compensation. This
was definitely sounding very benevolent. I thought
to myself what do I have to lose and enthusiastically
accepted the invitation. This decision is one I will never
regret.

During our first gathering we were asked to write
down a definition for what community meant to us. I
reflected on the definition of benevolent I saw in the
dictionary and quickly wrote the following: Community
is love in action. It means getting down in the dirt
with each other and sowing the seeds of sympathy and
understanding and generosity. In other words, building a
benevolent community.

I believe we are all community builders whether we know
it or not and "we're not meant to live life alone." As
the song *No Man Is an Island, written by John Whitney and
Alex Kramer,* points out:

I won't run, I will stay
I'm not leaving you
I know there's friction here
The struggle makes us new

I wish you never thought you had to go.
Wish you never thought you had to leave!
Together we can lift each other up, We can build
a shelter for the weak!

No man is an island, we can be found

No man is an island, let your guard down!

You don't have to fight me, I am for you

We're not meant to live life alone!

Building a benevolent community doesn't have to be
very complicated. You just have to allow yourself to be
vulnerable and open to others. Wherever two people meet,
the seeds of sympathy, understanding and generosity can
be sowed.

Delaware Retreat by Clint

A homeless man inspires a young soul.
A safe space is created in a corn crib and Martin's hand
guides her way.
Shades of color gather at the farmhouse.
Diversity and inclusion fill the rooms.
Cries for justice are made.
A selfless patriarch serves our needs.
Morning coffee warms the heart.
Bagels honor an ancient culture.
Hugs and books are shared.
A benevolent community goes forth.
We Shall Overcome.

 LORI ANN

Kathie:

Thoughts on My Participation in a Benevolent Community

I retired at the end of 2019, and my husband and I moved to our home near the beach. I grew up close to bays and the ocean. The ocean has always been a place of beauty and solace for me. I had never expected to live near it again, so I was delighted.

Our plan was to use this new chapter of life to travel, spend more time with my young nephews, adult children, and friends. I looked forward to a quieter life with less rushing. As an introvert, I knew I would be challenged to step out of my comfort zone to find conversation, connection, and community as I aged—hopefully with grace, acceptance, and meaning. As Parker Palmer notes, *"It doesn't matter how old we are, the search for meaning and purpose never ends."*

Little did I know that by March of 2020, life around the world would be slowed by COVID-19. At the same time, a deeply divisive political climate ignited smoldering anger about racial injustice, the consequences of unmet needs among many marginalized communities, and the rise of anti-Asian attacks after a sitting President called COVID-19 the "China virus." This introvert discovered that I needed connection even more than I had realized— even if it had to be virtual, through Zoom.

In 2021, I joined a Dialogue to Action group, a series of six meetings with strangers willing to engage in deep and sometimes difficult conversations about our own experiences with race. Always interested in social justice and curious about others' perspectives on the conflicts of the COVID-19 era, I found myself seeking company, knowledge, and conversation during a time of isolation. Happily, I was invited to join a follow-up group facilitated

by Lori Yadin and Natasha Warsaw. I have continued
to be part of a virtual Benevolent Community that has
expanded my understanding and, most importantly,
connected me with a wonderful group of people—
individuals with different backgrounds, willing to be
vulnerable, to share concerns, and to explore differing
perspectives and possible paths forward.

Having witnessed the unrest of the 1960s and gradual
progress in civil rights for people of color, women, and
the LGBTQ community, I had hoped protests would
be peaceful and would awaken a new generation to the
need to reckon with true American history - especially
the enduring impact of slavery on the Black community,
and the contributions of immigrants to American society.
Although concerned about the prevalence of screens in
our daily lives, I was grateful for the ways cell phones and
body cameras documented violence against people of
color and other marginalized groups.

Now, in 2025, I am observing a nation - and a world - in
turbulence. Each day, I read or hear fears of American
authoritarianism, witness growing food insecurity and
homelessness, and follow news reports about wars, racism,
antisemitism, Islamophobia, and hate crimes against
Asian and LGBTQ communities - or anyone perceived as
"other." Some say turbulence often precedes growth and
progress. For me, the unrest and violence brought both fear
and the beginnings of despair for humanity.

Being part of a Benevolent Community renewed my hope.
Through this community, I rediscovered Parker Palmer's
teachings and the lessons of communicating with those
who hold different perspectives—especially through the
"Circle of Trust" approach.

This format invites us to examine both conscious and
unconscious biases and to listen deeply to others' values

71

and beliefs with curiosity, wonder, and without judgment.

Connecting with others in this way inspired me to balance my quieter life with meaningful action. Never a particularly political person, I now contact my elected representatives with my concerns and occasionally volunteer for or donate to causes that advance human rights. I also chose to continue working part-time as a Social Worker/Therapist with cancer survivors, many of whom belong to marginalized groups and are now navigating healthcare systems—places where I have witnessed both great compassion and deep-seated bias.

Throughout my life, I have tried, though not always perfectly - to treat others with kindness and respect. Even as a shy child, I was fascinated by people's different beliefs and interests. The Benevolent Community encourages that same curiosity and wonder, while also reminding us of our shared humanity. The Benevolent Community keeps my hope alive.

Shared by Kathie:

Harold Kushner's *A Prayer for the World* captures the vision I hold:

A PRAYER FOR THE WORLD
Let the rain come and wash away
the ancient grudges, the bitter hatreds
held and nurtured over generations.
Let the rain wash away the memory
of the hurt, the neglect.
Then let the sun come out and
fill the sky with rainbows.
Let the warmth of the sun heal us
wherever we are broken.
Let it burn away the fog so that
we can see each other clearly—

so that we can see beyond labels,
beyond accents, gender, or skin color.
Let the warmth and brightness
of the sun melt our selfishness,
so that we can share the joys and
feel the sorrows of our neighbors.
And let the light of the sun
be so strong that we will see all
people as our neighbors.
Let the earth, nourished by rain,
bring forth flowers
to surround us with beauty.
And let the mountains teach our hearts
to reach upward to heaven.
Amen.

Sally:

Lessons Learned:

A Few Reflections from a Remarkable Year of Intentionally Creating Benevolent Community

1. Community is not a goal to be achieved; it is a gift to be received.
2. All gifts have shadows.
3. Let the Beauty you love be what you do. (Rumi)
4. Embrace paradox.
5. Practice soft eyes.
6. No fixing.
7. Laugh often.
8. Cry often and appreciate the value of tears. (After all, even scientific research tells us there is a difference in the chemistry of tears of grief and tears from cutting an onion, and the former cleanses the body of impurities.)
9. The words Listen and Silent are made up of the same letters, in a different order.
10. Be. Be still. Take time for yourself.
11. Be kind to yourself.
12. Be kind to others. But you don't have to say yes to every request or entertain them —or feed them — or return their phone calls — or take their advice — or even answer the door when they ring the bell.
13. Tell the Truth — but tell it slant.
14. Ask for help.
15. Some things have to be believed to be seen: Know that benevolent community is possible.

Ouida z'l:

I have been drawn to and deeply touched by the writing of Paker J. Palmer, The Center for Courage and Renewal, and Benevolent Community Retreats. Here is a poignant quote from Parker that seems foundational to all this work:

"If we are willing to embrace the challenge of becoming whole, we can't do it alone. We all need other people to invite, amplify, and help us listen to our inner teacher. We all need trustworthy relationships — tenacious communities of support — if we hope to sustain the journey towards wholeness."

Parker J. Palmer

 LORI ANN

Candy:

Reflections on our Benevolent Community:

I barely made it into this group. I was watching for a retreat I could afford, it was during the pandemic, and I found this zoom group and signed up. I had read some of Parker Palmer's books, so I had some idea of what it would be like. The first night, we were divided into pairs. The lady that I was matched with - out accomplished me in many ways, and I felt intimidated. Later, she talked about what she had been told about "people like me" all her life, and that she was pleased to learn that what she had been told was wrong. That in truth we were people who can learn to love each other. Once the pandemic had been managed, we met at an in-person Retreat, and it was great, seeing everyone and knowing them immediately was a real treat. I learned a lot about civil rights and racism from the individuals and the personal stories shared, and this interest still guides me in my church group and politics. I learned, "From the greatest chaos comes the greatest change." This concept has come up in many different ways since, personally, spiritually, and in current events — chaos does not mean the end is here. It could mean we are about to learn and grow and move forward in our development. Knowing this and that I have a benevolent community to connect with helps me to let go of the panic and fear, and really look at what's going on with curiosity. What's next?

Natasha:

Planting Seeds of Compassion in Education

I began my career as a teacher at the dawn of No Child Left Behind, when education was increasingly shaped by standards, numbers, and high-stakes testing. Over time, the emphasis on data began to eclipse what I saw as the heart of teaching: guiding young people not only in their learning, but also in their growth as empathetic, compassionate human beings.

The rise of cell phones and later social media further complicated this work. While these tools offered new forms of connection, they also introduced new layers of isolation, comparison, and distraction that made it harder to help young people become grounded, whole, and openhearted.

Now, twenty-five years later, I look at our country and see how disconnection has taken root. Too often, neighbors, families, and friends struggle to listen with openness or hold space for perspectives different from their own. Judgment and division dominate where kindness and curiosity could lead. Yet I believe the path to healing is still within reach—through practices of compassion, empathy, and benevolence.

Education has a powerful role to play in this healing. Classrooms at every level—from kindergarten to college—can be intentional spaces where students learn to trust, listen without judgment, and practice dialogue rooted in respect and openness. When schools extend benevolent community to young people, they offer more than academic preparation; they offer the foundation for resilient, compassionate citizenship.

As an educator and facilitator, I believe the seeds of lasting

 LORI ANN

change lie in our youth. By creating spaces for them to show up as their whole selves, by modeling empathy and compassion, and by cultivating a culture of openness, we prepare a generation capable of reshaping our world with courage, kindness, and love.

Essential Question:

How are you seeing compassion and empathy show up—or fall short—in education and in our communities today?

What practices have you found helpful in creating spaces of openness and belonging?

Invitation to Practice

Start a community conversation with colleagues, neighbors and friends about how we can extend benevolent community to the next generation, together.

Lori's words

<u>The Weight of What's Missing</u>

It seems our sensing
is sharper in absence
than in presence…

The streets we have built
are paved with what is missing—
kindness, safety, compassion,
empathy, goodwill, generosity,
integrity.

We name the things we lack
as treasures to be obtained,
not ways of being
to be lived.

We forget
that all we need
is here.

We choose what to remember,
what to hold as sacred,
whether to strip away humanity
or restore it.

We choose how we walk in this world—

 LORI ANN

What we lift up,
what we let fall,
who we become,
what we will stand for,
whom we will deny
or defend.

We choose to hate.
We choose to love.

We choose the presence we invite into our lives—
And in that choice,
we decide
what will be
absent.

-Lori Ann

Berry, W. (2013). This day: Collected & new Sabbath poems.
Counterpoint Press.

Berry, W. (2015). Our only world: Ten essays. Counterpoint Press.

Reference List:

The following authors, thinkers, and works have inspired, informed, and enriched the ideas within Rooted in Humanity: Reclaiming Benevolence in Support of a Community's Coming of Age.

Some are quoted directly; others have shaped the spirit, language, and vision of this work.

Angelou, M. (1993). *Phenomenal woman: Four poems celebrating women*. Random House.

Berry, W. (2013). This day: Collected & new Sabbath poems. Counterpoint Press.

Berry, W. (2015). Our only world: Ten essays. Counterpoint Press

Brooks, D. (2019). *The second mountain: The quest for a moral life*. Random House.

Brooks, G. (1960). *The Bean Eaters*. Harper & Row.

Brown, A. M. (2017). *Emergent strategy: Shaping change, changing worlds*. AK Press.

Brown, A. M. (2021). *Holding change: The way of emergent strategy facilitation and mediation*. AK Press.

Buber, M. (1970). *I and Thou* (W. Kaufmann, Trans.). Charles Scribner's Sons. (Original work published 1923)

Ellis, D. (n.d.). *The five-fold path to healing™*. [Self-published resource].

Frank, A. (1995). *The diary of a young girl* (D. Massotty, Trans.). Bantam. (Original work published 1947)

Gandhi, M. (1993). *An autobiography: The story of my experiments with truth*. Beacon Press.

Gilpin, L. (2010). The two-headed calf. In The Hocus Pocus of the Universe. Boston: Houghton Mifflin.

Hafiz. (1999). The gift: Poems by Hafiz, the great Sufi Master (D. Ladinsky, Trans.). Penguin Compass.

Halifax, J. (2018). *Standing at the edge: Finding freedom where fear and courage meet*. Flatiron Books.

Hare, S. Z. (2016). *The ElderGarten*. Coastal Carolina Press.

Heschel, A. J. (1951). *The Sabbath*. Farrar, Straus and Giroux.
Heschel, A. J. (1955). *God in search of man: A philosophy of Judaism*. Farrar, Straus and Giroux.

Iyer, D. (2022). *Social change now: A guide for reflection and connection*. The Social Change Map Project.

Kimmerer, R. W. (2013). *Braiding sweetgrass: Indigenous wisdom, scientific knowledge, and the teachings of plants*. Milkweed Editions.

King, M. L., Jr. (1963). *Strength to love*. Harper & Row.

Kushner, H. S. (1995). *A prayer for the world*. In *Who needs God*. Simon & Schuster.

Levinas, E. (1969). *Totality and infinity: An essay on exteriority* (A. Lingis, Trans.). Duquesne University Press.

Levinas, E. (1985). *Ethics and infinity: Conversations with Philippe Nemo* (R. A. Cohen, Trans.). Duquesne University Press.

Palmer, P. J. (1983). *To know as we are known: Education as a spiritual journey*. Harper & Row.

Palmer, P. J. (1998). *The courage to teach: Exploring the inner landscape of a teacher's life*. Jossey-Bass.

Palmer, P. J. (2000). *Let your life speak: Listening for the voice of vocation*. Jossey-Bass.

Palmer, P. J. (2004). *A hidden wholeness: The journey toward an undivided life*. Jossey-Bass.

Palmer, P. J. (2011). *Healing the heart of democracy: The courage to create a politics worthy of the human spirit*. Jossey-Bass.

powell, j. a. (2012). *Racing to justice: Transforming our conceptions of self and other to build an inclusive society*. Indiana University Press.

powell, j. a. (2024). *Belonging without othering: How we
save ourselves and the world*. Berrett-Koehler Publishers.

Remen, R. N. (1996). *Kitchen table wisdom: Stories that heal*.
Riverhead Books.

Rilke, R. M. (2004). *Letters to a young poet* (M. D. Herter Norton,
Trans.). W. W. Norton & Company. (Original work published 1929)

Rogers, F. (2005). Life's journeys according to Mister Rogers:
Things to remember along the way. Hyperion.

Rogers, Jim R. Rogers (2012) The Incredible Importance of Effective Parenting: Plain Talk About Raising Children From a Concerned Field Worker. Prose Press.
Rogers, Jim R. Rogers (2012) Starts and Stops Along the Way. Poetry. Prose Press

Sacks, J. (2005). *To heal a fractured world: The ethics of responsibility*. Schocken Books.

Schulman Yadin, Lori Ann. (2017). Moving through life: thresholds of past, present, and future. Prose Press.

Solnit, R. (2016). *Hope in the dark: Untold histories, wild possibilities*. Haymarket Books.

Stevenson, B. (2014). *Just mercy: A story of justice and redemp-
tion*. Spiegel & Grau.

Tippett, K. (2016). *Becoming wise: An inquiry into the mystery and
art of living*. Penguin Press.

Weingarten, E. (2020). *How to fall in love with questions*. [Publi-
cation details if available].

Williams, R. (1983). *Keywords: A vocabulary of culture and society*. Oxford University Press

Lori Schulman Yadin (Lori Ann) is an Experiential Educator, Retreat and Workshop Facilitator, Leadership Coach, and Writer. She is the Founder of Create Safe Space, Inc., a human centered nonprofit dedicated to cultivating thriving environments that inspire healthy relationships, uplift the spirit, and grow communities rooted in dignity, integrity, empathy, belonging, and generosity of heart.

Lori's life has been shaped by listening to stories. As a child, her most formative friendship was with Hank, a homeless veteran who lived, for a short while, in the woods near her home. His wisdom and humanity sparked her lifelong devotion to sacred listening, compassion, and creating spaces of safety and trust. This devotion continues to guide her work with individuals and communities, and her current focus, The Benevolent Community Initiative Circles and Retreats.

She is an Independent Facilitator affiliated with the Center for Courage & Renewal®, trained by Parker J. Palmer and the Center's leadership team. A lifelong learner, Lori holds degrees in Experiential Education, and Landscape Design with a focus on history of land design and human relationship to place from George Washington University, and advanced studies in Educational Psychology and Diversity. She received her Executive Coaching Certification from Case Western Reserve University's Weatherhead School of Management, a program grounded in emotional intelligence and completed pro-social human development training at the Greater Good Science Center, UC Berkeley. Her writing (published under Lori Ann) **includes** a book of poetry, *moving through life: thresholds of past, present, and future,* and *Rooted in Humanity: Reclaiming Our Future Through Benevolent Community,* and her first Children's Book – *One, Two,*

Three, BENE: A Wish for a Kinder World. In addition,
Lori, with contributions from her friend and colleague,
Natasha Warsaw, created a curriculum as a guide to
those wishing to begin a Benevolent Community Circle –
entitled, Living A Year of Essential Questions: Reclaiming
Humanity through Benevolent Community in Support of
a Community's Coming of Age, and a companion journal,
Rooted In Humanity - A Journal for Living with Integrity,
Benevolence, and Community, that can be used with the
curriculum, book, or as a thought partner for personal
reflection. Lori envisions a world where holding one
another's dignity is at the core of our shared humanity.

Lori, who is a native to Washington, D.C., is now living in
Savannah, Georgia, in a small neighborhood bordering the
Herb River Marsh and sheltered by a historic 500-year-
old oak tree. Lori continues to draw inspiration from
waterways, gardens, lived experiences, and the bountiful
gifts of nature. She treasures time with her children
and grandchildren, walks with her dogs, and the joy of
simple acts of loving-kindness. Lori keeps a quote book
with quotes that inspire and provide hope in her pursuit
of repairing the brokenness of our world. One of her
favorites is this one by Fred Rogers.

"We live in a world in which we need to share
responsibility. It's easy to say, "It's not my child, not my
community, not my world, not my problem." Then there
are those who see the need and respond. I consider those
people my heroes." – Fred Rogers

Natasha Warsaw: With more than two decades in education, Natasha Warsaw has walked alongside students, teachers, and communities in ways that center both learning and humanity. She began her career as a middle school English and Social Studies teacher in DC Public Schools, teaching a wide range of learners and drawing inspiration from her own lineage as a fifth-generation educator. Her deep commitment to equity and to honoring Black life and history continues to shape her belief that every student deserves an education that reflects and affirms their identity.

Natasha went on to join the New Leaders Principal Training Program, serving in leadership roles in both DC Public and Charter Schools. She later founded Sustainable Futures Public Charter School, which is transitioning into a private, tuition-free micro school for students aged sixteen to twenty-four. This space is designed to provide identity-responsive, restorative learning environments where students are encouraged to thrive.

In her current role as a coach and consultant, Natasha partners with schools and organizations across the country to reimagine what education can be. As a trained facilitator with the Center for Courage & Renewal, she helps leaders, educators, and communities show up as their whole selves in every area of their lives.

Her approach is grounded in the understanding that empathy and compassion are not add-ons, but essential practices in education and in leadership.

Natasha's work is rooted in a vision of transformative,
sustainable futures for all students—drawing strength
from the resilience of Black communities and the belief
that learning spaces can be places of wholeness and
belonging. Beyond her professional commitments, she
finds joy in reading, kayaking, and spending time with her
family and pets.

Summary

Rooted in Humanity is a heartfelt invitation to remember who we are beneath the noise of a fractured world. It is a love letter to our shared humanity and a call to awaken the benevolence that lives, quietly but steadfastly, at the roots of every community.

Through story, reflection, and timeless questions, Lori Ann weaves a tapestry of memory and possibility—reminding us that communities, like people, have seasons of growth, moments of reckoning, and the chance to come of age with wisdom and grace.

This book is for all who long to belong, to build, to heal. It is for those who believe that generosity of heart can change the arc of our shared future, and that in learning to see and hear one another anew, we can cultivate spaces where trust grows deep and compassion lights the way.

Rooted in Humanity is not just a book—it is an offering. A lantern held high. A gentle, steady reminder that together, we can envision and build communities worthy of the gift we all share -
Our Humanity.

www.ingramcontent.com/pod-product-compliance
Lightning Source LLC
Chambersburg PA
CBHW061709120626
46550CB00003B/1156